Uncharted, Unexplored, and Unexplained

Scientific Advancements of the 19th Century

J. J. Thomson
and the
Discovery of Electrons

Mitchell Lane
PUBLISHERS

P.O. Box 196
Hockessin, Delaware 19707

Uncharted, Unexplored, and Unexplained

Scientific Advancements of the 19th Century

Titles in the Series

Visit us on the web: www.mitchelllane.com
Comments? email us: mitchelllane@mitchelllane.com

Uncharted, Unexplored, and Unexplained

Scientific Advancements of the 19th Century

J. J. Thomson
and the
Discovery of Electrons

Josepha Sherman

Uncharted, Unexplored, and Unexplained

Scientific Advancements of the 19th Century

Mitchell Lane
PUBLISHERS

Printing   1   2   3   4   5   6   7   8
        Library of Congress Cataloging-in-Publication Data
Sherman, Josepha.
        J. J. Thomson and the discovery of electrons / by Josepha Sherman.
                p. cm. — (Uncharted, unexplored, and unexplained)
        Includes bibliographical references and index.
        ISBN 1-58415-370-9 (lib. bound)
1. Thomson, J. J. (Joseph John), Sir, 1856-1940. 2. Physicists—Great Britain
Biography—Juvenile literature. I. Title. II. Series.
QC16.T45S48 2005
530'.092—dc22
[B]

                                                        2004024615

ABOUT THE AUTHOR: Josepha Sherman is a professional fantasy and science fiction writer, a *Star Trek* novelist, a children's writer, and a nonfiction writer with over 60 books in print and over 150 short stories. She is also a professional folklorist and editor. In addition, she is a native New Yorker, has a degree in archaeology, loves to tinker with computers, follows the NY Mets ("wait till next year!"), and is a horse whisperer who has had a new foal fall asleep on her foot!

PHOTO CREDITS: Cover, pp. 1, 3—Corbis; pp. 6, 10—Getty Images; p. 12—Hulton/Archive; pp. 14, 16, 20—Corbis; p. 28—Photo Researchers; pp. 30, 32—Corbis; p. 36—Getty Images; p. 39—Corbis

PUBLISHER'S NOTE: This story is based on the author's extensive research, which she believes to be accurate. Documentation of such research is contained on page 46.

The internet sites referenced herein were active as of the publication date. Due to the fleeting nature of some web sites, we cannot guarantee they will all be active when you are reading this book.

Uncharted, Unexplored, and Unexplained

Scientific Advancements of the 19th Century

J. J. Thomson
and the Discovery of Electrons

J. J. was a physics pioneer who discovered the electron. This ground-breaking discovery revolutionized the theories of atomic structure.

1

The Professor
Who Liked Questions

It was a warm, pleasant springtime in New Haven, Connecticut in June, 1903. Scientists were gathering eagerly at a lecture hall on the campus of Yale University.

"The Silliman Lectures are going to be very different this year," one scientist said to several others about the annual presentations which featured world-famous scientists. "They should be fascinating, too."

"That's right," a second scientist agreed. "Professor Joseph John Thomson has come all the way from England to speak here."

"That's so formal a name!" the first man said with a laugh. "The professor prefers to be called J. J."

"Do you suppose he'll speak about his findings on the atom?" asked the second.

"Perhaps he even has worked out a true model of one," suggested a third.

None of the scientists noticed a young boy who was eagerly listening to them. He was the son of a science professor, one of the men attending the lectures. Though the youngster was only seven, he already knew that he wanted to learn more about science. And the thought of hearing Professor Joseph Thomson, no, no, J. J., was so exciting he couldn't stand still. He wanted so much to attend the lectures!

"Don't be ridiculous!" the boy's father exclaimed. "You're only seven! You won't understand a word the professor says."

"But I want to try!" the boy cried. "I have so many questions I want to ask him."

"I said no. You are too young, and I will not have you bothering such an important man. And that is that."

Sadly, the boy sat down outside the lecture hall. He'd just have to wait, and hope that maybe his father would tell him something about the talk.

Time passed. More time passed. The lecture must have been going on for a long time. Or maybe the famous professor was being asked questions. Maybe even the questions he had wanted to ask.

"I beg your pardon," a man's voice said. It had an English accent.

The boy looked up. The man was tall, with a high forehead and a thin mustache. Sharp eyes gleamed from behind his glasses. "You're Professor Thomson!" the boy cried.

The professor sat down beside him. "Indeed I am. Now, I understand you had difficulty attending my lecture."

"Uh, yes, sir. My father said that I'm too young. I'm only seven, you see."

"But you do have questions."

"Yes, sir, I do."

"Very well, then, boy. Ask away! How else are you to learn?"

Much later, the boy ran to meet his father. "I don't know why you said I wouldn't understand Professor Thomson. He just spoke to me, and I understood every word," he said.

What his father said to that, nobody knows. But Professor J. J. Thomson never left anyone's questions unanswered.[1]

Queen Victoria

England had a woman ruler, Queen Victoria, for nearly two-thirds of the nineteenth century. She took the throne in 1837, and remained queen until her death in 1901. She was so strong and stern a ruler that she gave her name to that time period: the Victorian Age.

In some ways it was a strange time. Certain words were not allowed in polite society. Imagine having to call a table leg a "table limb" or having a "chest of chicken" for dinner. It was also a time of increasing industrialization. More machines were in use every year, making life easier for many people. But it was also a time of terrible air pollution. The main source of fuel for most of these machines was soft coal, which gives off a great deal of smoke. At the same time, the arts did very well. Nineteenth century England produced great writers, painters, and architects.

The nineteenth century was also the dawn of the science known as physics, the study of how things work. One of the most important developments came in 1871 when work began on the Cavendish Laboratory. Finished in 1873, it was named in honor of Henry Cavendish, an English scientist who had discovered hydrogen during the previous century. Its original purpose was to serve as a laboratory to aid in the teaching of physics at Cambridge University. It soon became a world-famous center for physics experiments.

The Cavendish Laboratory is still very active today. Students can do research on sciences such as biology, astrophysics—the study of what space and the stars and planets are made of—high-energy physics, including nuclear power, low-temperature and high-temperature physics, and other fields that tell us how things actually work. The quality of the work that is, and has been, conducted there is indicated by the fact that 28 scientists who have done their research at the Cavendish Laboratory have been awarded Nobel Prizes.

9

J. J. was born in Manchester, England on December 18, 1856. The illustration above depicts Manchester and one of its canals in the 1800s. Today over 2.5 million people live in Manchester making it the second largest city—London is the largest—in England.

2

The Bookseller's Son

On December 18, 1856, Mr. Joseph Thomson closed his antiquarian bookstore, which is a bookstore selling only old titles. It was located in Cheetham, a suburb of the city of Manchester, England. He wanted to be at the side of his wife, Emma. She was giving birth to their first child. While Mr. Thomson waited nervously for the baby to be born, he might have been thinking that the new arrival could be the third generation of Thomsons who would run the little bookstore. His own father had come down to Manchester from Scotland to open it. Joseph himself, the second Thomson, was the current owner. If the child was a boy, Mr. Thomson thought, he would surely inherit the bookstore.

The child was indeed a son. His happy parents named him Joseph, like his father. They added a second name, John. Even so, it still was a little confusing to have two Joseph Thomsons in the family. The boy soon picked up a nickname, J. J., which was short for Joseph John. He liked it so much that he kept the nickname all his life.

Growing up in a bookstore as he did, young J. J. would have played among books even before he could read. So would his younger brother Frederick, who was born four years later. Of course the two boys would have been too young to realize that their father was not a very healthy man. But J. J. would have known right away that his father was very proud of his sons. He was especially proud of J. J.'s quick mind.

In fact, J. J. outgrew what the local school could teach him when he was only fourteen. The teenager was so good at mathematics by this point that his father had to admit that it would be wrong to waste such talent by working as a bookseller. There were engineers in the Thomson family, designers and manufacturers of machine engines. J. J.'s father thought that engineering, which needed a

In J. J.'s day, locomotives ran on steam power. Their steam engines were designed and built by special engineering firms. J. J. might have been apprenticed to one of them.

good knowledge of mathematics, would be a more suitable job for his son.

In those days, the middle of the nineteenth century, it was still common for boys to be apprenticed to become masters of the profession they were trying to learn. The boys would serve as assistants to the master, helping out with whatever tasks had to be done. At the same time they would learn the skills they needed to perform the job. Joseph Thomson wanted J. J. to be apprenticed to an engineering firm, a company that specialized in the manufacture of railroad locomotives. But there was a long waiting list for would-be apprentices at the firm. Also, J. J.'s parents were probably shocked to learn how much they would have to pay in apprenticeship fees.

Joseph Thomson didn't want his son to waste his time waiting for an apprentice position to open up, so he sent J. J. to Owens College in 1871. Founded in 1851, Owens College had quickly gained a reputation for being a good school. In fact, it was so fine a school that it later became Manchester University and then the Victoria University of Manchester. It still exists and is now officially known as the University of Manchester.

In J. J.'s time, the area surrounding Owens College was a crowded, rundown part of Manchester. There was little room for the school itself. The students were often crowded together in small classrooms. In fact, the engineering department was located in what had once been a stable. However, the conditions weren't all bad. As J. J. commented later, "The cramped space was not without its advantages. We were so closely packed that it was very easy for us to get to know each other."[1] J. J. was a rather shy boy at the time. The fact that he couldn't hide in a corner and had to make friends right away must have helped him get over his shyness.

At Owens College, J. J. studied engineering, physics, mathematics and chemistry. It was an exciting place for a young

13

James Joule was one of the important scientists who lived in Manchester when J. J. was in school. Joule was one of the first scientists to work on theories of energy. He made the important discovery that energy cannot be created or lost.

teenager to be, especially one who was growing more and more fascinated by science. In addition to what he could learn at school, J. J. would have quickly realized that Manchester had its own noted science organization. Known as the Literary and Philosophical Society, it had been founded in 1781. Philosophy in the middle of the nineteenth century included what is now called theoretical physics, the basic study of how things work.

To his delight, J. J. was even introduced to famous scientists such as James Joule while he was in Manchester. In 1845, Joule had discovered that energy produced heat, and that an equal amount of energy created an equal amount of heat. Joule's experiments proved that energy can be transformed but not created or lost. This was the law of conservation of energy. It was a discovery that J. J. would use in a few years.

But after J. J. had studied for two years at Owens College, tragedy struck the Thomson family. His father had never been a healthy man. Now his illness—the records fail to mention what kind it was—grew suddenly worse, and he died without warning.

In addition to the family's grief, they had to face a painful fact. There was now almost no money. They could not even think about having J. J. apprenticed. That would cost them far too much. Emma Thomson, left with two young sons and no husband, was forced to sell the bookstore. She moved her family to a small house near the college, and managed to find the money to keep J. J. in school. He also was able to get a small scholarship, which helped a great deal.

At last the Thomson family was able to settle into their new lives. Things worked out very well for J. J. after that. Even though he earned his engineering degree by the end of his third year at Owens College, he knew he wasn't meant to be an engineer. If he'd been apprenticed to an engineer, though, there wouldn't have been a choice. He would have to work as an engineer to pay back the apprentice fee.

J. J. had also earned another scholarship, one that let him stay on at Owens for another year to study the two subjects that he'd really come to love. These were physics and mathematics.

His enthusiasm for science almost cut his career short. While working alone in a laboratory one day, J. J. combined mercury and iodine in a glass flask and heated the mixture over a flame. This procedure was supposed to create a tiny, controlled explosion—but it didn't. Nothing happened. He waited. Still nothing happened. J. J. reported afterwards that he then made a very foolish mistake—the same sort of foolish mistake people make when they pick up lit firecrackers to see why the firecrackers didn't explode. As he wrote later, "I held [the flask] up...to see what was the matter, when it suddenly exploded; the hot compound of mercury and iodine went over my face and pieces of glass flew into my eyes...For some days it was doubtful whether I should recover my sight. Mercifully, I did so."[2]

Trinity College is part of Cambridge University. This is a modern photograph, but the buildings would have looked the same in J. J.'s school days. They were built in the early eighteenth century.

He never made such a dangerous mistake again. In fact, from then on, J. J. avoided doing experiments whenever he could. He knew that he was too clumsy for any work that required delicate handling. When he had to do experiments, he often wasn't very successful, as notes recorded by one of his professors indicate. These notes include the following entries:

"Tues 13 Jan. Mr. Thomson made some experiments in measuring electrical resistances but not very successful."

"Thurs 5 Feb. Mr. Thomson made some readings of the apparatus for estimating electromotive force of a battery but the needle did not work well and results not worth recording."

"Mon 9 Feb. Mr. Thomson proceeded with experiment for electromotive force of a battery but was unable to obtain a good action of the needle."

"Fri 13 Feb. Mr. Thomson made another attempt to get the electromotive force of a battery, but could not get the needle to act well."[3]

But these problems—not even the accident that nearly cost him his sight—didn't take away his love of science. J. J.'s professors quickly saw his brilliance. One of them was Thomas Barker,

J. J.'s professor of mathematics. He encouraged the boy to apply for a scholarship at Trinity College. Trinity College was a very important part of Cambridge University, one that had a top reputation in the sciences. It was also one of the most difficult schools to get into. The competition for the scholarship that would let him attend was fierce, and J. J. was turned down in 1875. But he refused to give up. J. J. tried again in 1876, and this time he won the scholarship. It marked the beginning of an association with Cambridge that would continue for the rest of his life.

The most important goal for mathematics students at Trinity was to become First Wrangler by doing well in a highly difficult test known as the Mathematical Tripos. They were named after the tripos, or the three-legged stool that had once been used during the test. Students usually needed several years of preparation and coaching to prepare for them. The Mathematical Tripos lasted for nine days and covered every type of mathematics, which is what made it so difficult. Few students were at the top in their class for every type, and even fewer of them could last nine days of testing. Adding to the difficulty of the test was the timing. The Tripos were normally held during the cold month of January and the tests were taken in unheated rooms. According to some reports, the ink that students used would sometimes freeze. J. J. overcame the obstacles and graduated in 1880 as Second Wrangler, second of all the mathematics students.

Even with all the pressures of preparing for the tests and going to his classes, J. J. still had enough time to send off three of his papers on mathematics. They were published in a scientific journal, *Messenger of Mathematics*, in 1877, 1878 and 1879.

Finishing second in such a challenging a test was quite an accomplishment. Thanks to his high ranking, J. J. received a fellowship from Trinity College. This award allowed him to do his own research without having to worry about money. J. J. was now 24, and delighted at the thought of receiving an award to do exactly what he had wanted to do all along.

In nineteenth century physics, one of the major theories accepted by all the scientists was that energy was always conserved. This had nothing to do with the modern idea of saving energy by turning out lights. The theory of the conservation of energy meant that energy could appear in many forms, including electricity and magnetism, but it could never be created or destroyed.

J. J. wondered about the details of that theory. What if energy didn't change from one form to another? What if it was constantly being transferred from one place to another? Could it be that all energy was actually kinetic energy, which is energy that is constantly in motion?

The questions weren't easy to answer. J. J. spent the next three years happily designing mathematical equations that he hoped would reveal more about the nature of energy.

Everybody knows that energy exists. We hear that a runner "ran out of energy," or that one brand of flashlight battery "has more energy" than another. We read about "energy-saving" machines.

But what is energy? Scientists define energy as the ability of something to do work (such as the force that lets an athlete run) or produce heat (such as the force that starts a fire).

A Volcano—a type of energy

There are two major kinds of energy: kinetic energy and potential energy. Kinetic energy is the energy of something in motion. A thrown baseball flies through the air because of its kinetic energy. Kinetic art is art (usually a sculpture with many parts) that moves.

Potential energy, which is also known as stored energy, is the opposite of kinetic energy. Some of the most common forms of potential energy are in food—which will be turned into energy when it's eaten—and in a flashlight, which only emits light, radiant energy, if it's switched on.

What may appear to be other kinds of energy are really forms of either kinetic or potential energy. For instance, sunlight is called radiant energy because it radiates from the sun. But it is actually kinetic energy since the sunlight is in motion. It's created by a flow of tiny particles in straight lines.

Another familiar form of kinetic energy is thermal energy, or heat. The heat from a fire or from a radiator is an example of thermal energy. Heat that comes from the earth, such as the heat from volcanoes, is called geothermal energy. Unlike radiant energy, thermal energy is caused by the vibration and movement of particles inside a substance.

Nuclear energy is one form of potential energy, as the energy is stored in the nucleus of an atom. Chemical energy, such as propane and natural gas, is also potential energy. So is hydropower, the water stored behind a dam.

19

In 1884, J. J. was chosen to be the Cavendish Professor of
Experimental Physics at Cambridge University. Although
he was inexperienced in doing experiments, he learned
quickly and presided over a flourishing physics program.

3

Professor Thomson

In 1882, while he was still a student at Trinity College, J. J. was selected for an assistant lectureship in mathematics. In the United States we would call him a teaching assistant or an assistant professor. From 1882 on, J. J. taught classes and continued his research. Those two jobs kept him pretty busy. But he enjoyed doing both of them.

Every two years, Cambridge University awarded the Adams Prize in science for the best scholarly paper. The topic for the paper was picked in advance by the university board and then given out to those entering the contest. In 1882, the topic was "The movement of liquid in a closed space."

J. J. won the prize with his paper, "A Treatise on the Motion of Vortex Rings." A vortex is a whirlpool, a circular swirling of liquid. J. J. was interested in the way the atoms making up a liquid might move in a vortex. He was curious about the energy that might be produced.

While teaching and doing his research, J. J. was also taking courses in physics at another branch of Cambridge University, the Cavendish Laboratory. The Cavendish Laboratory had been founded in 1871 in memory of another scientist, Henry Cavendish. The laboratory was designed to be both a part of the university and a research laboratory for experiments in physics and chemistry.

The head of the Cavendish Laboratory received the title of the Cavendish Professor of Experimental Physics. The first Cavendish Professor was James Clerk Maxwell. He had workmen place a Biblical quote from Psalm 111 above the main door to the laboratory: "The works of the Lord are great/Studied by all who have pleasure in them."

Professor Maxwell was an important physicist who was fascinated by natural forces. He was the first to create the basic equations of electromagnetism, the force that is electricity and magnetism together. Sadly, Professor Maxwell died of cancer in 1879 at the age of 48.

The second Cavendish Professor of Experimental Physics, who was asked by the laboratory to take over after Maxwell's death, was John William Strutt. He is better known by his title, Lord Rayleigh. Lord Rayleigh was highly respected by other physicists and famous for his studies of acoustics, which is the science of sound. But he resigned in 1884 to devote all his time to his own research and to his active membership in several important scientific organizations.

For the first time in the Cavendish Laboratory's history, a real election was held to choose the third Cavendish Professor of Experimental Physics. There was a long list of candidates for the post. J. J. was one of them. To the surprise of many people, he won the election.

At first, not everyone was happy about J. J.'s election. He was only 28 in 1884, and some of the scientists thought that he was too young to take over such an important post. One Cavendish tutor commented that "Things [have] come to a pretty pass when boys [are] made Professors."[1]

Another issue also bothered them. Lord Rayleigh said, "My doubt was whether Thomson should be the professor of experimental physics. He had done very little experimenting."[2]

It was true that J. J. didn't have much experience in performing physics experiments. Perhaps he'd taken the experience of that exploding flask hitting him in the eyes as a warning. He wasn't too sure that he was doing the right thing by accepting the post, either. J. J. wrote that he "felt like a fisherman who...had...hooked a fish much too heavy for him to land."[3] He even got so dizzy during his first lecture that he almost passed out in front of his students. But J. J. survived that first day, and went on to give other lectures without any problems.

The laboratory in which J. J. was supposed to work on his experiments was still fairly new, less than fifteen years old. J. J. might have been a little worried about doing damage. After all, he was never very good at doing experiments. J. J. freely admitted that he was just plain clumsy. As one of his student assistants, H. F. Newall, noted, "J. J. was very awkward with his fingers, and I found it very necessary not to encourage him to handle the instruments! But he was very helpful in talking over the way in which he thought things ought to go."[4]

That turned out to be J. J.'s real strength as a professor. He was very good at helping students learn and liked to share his enthusiasm for science. J. J. was also apparently a terrific lecturer. He didn't make the mistakes of other teachers. J. J. never talked too fast or tried to cover too much information in too short a time. The slower students could keep up, while the brighter students weren't bored. It helped that J. J. had a strong, clear voice and a good sense of humor—and that he genuinely liked his students. He was interested in the work of all the young researchers at the Cavendish. He would check on how they were doing every day and make suggestions when they were needed.

The students liked him, too. J. J. constantly received letters from graduates saying how much they had enjoyed studying with him, and how much he'd helped them. They even wrote funny songs about him, praising his science—and his sense of humor. He in turn wrote some funny verses about himself and his work. Some of these verses were parodies. A parody is a close imitation of the style of a literary or musical work, usually intended to be funny. One of his parody songs is given here in part. It is about ions, a particular form of atoms with a positive or negative electrical charge. J. J.'s song is about taking parts of atoms away and recombining them—putting those parts together again in different ways.

IONS MINE (sung to the tune of "My Darling Clementine")
In the dusty lab'ratory
'Mid the coils and wax and twine
There the atoms in their glory
Ionize and recombine.
(Chorus):
Oh my darlings! Oh my darlings!
Oh my darling ions mine!
You are lost and gone forever
When just once you recombine![5]

Songs such as these served two purposes. J. J. and his students found them funny. The humorous words and familiar tunes also helped students to remember the science behind the songs.

Of course, most of J. J.'s writing was much more serious. As an important university professor, he was expected to publish significant scientific works. In 1886, his first book, *Application of Dynamics to Physics and Chemistry*, made its appearance. More books were to come.

J. J. soon found himself involved in an important social change. Before the nineteenth century, it was very rare for a woman to be allowed to get any advanced education. Few women were allowed to learn more than the basic elements of reading and writing. By the time J. J. was attending college, some women were getting at least partial college educations. But up until the time of J. J.'s administration as professor at the Cavendish Laboratory, no women were allowed to attend advanced university classes. At first J. J. wasn't so sure that the rule should be changed. He wondered if mixed classes of men and women would be too distracting for everyone. But he finally decided that anyone who wanted an advanced course in anything as difficult as physics deserved a chance. He agreed that admitting women was a good idea. In 1887, J. J. voted with other members of the Cavendish Laboratory staff to allow women into the Cavendish Laboratory.

One of the first women to take advantage of this opportunity was a young lady named Rose Paget. She attended some of J. J.'s lectures and wanted to do research. On October 15, 1888, J. J. sent her a brief note. "Dear Miss Paget," it read, "I think I have found a subject which you could work at with advantage, and if you will come to the Laboratory any afternoon after 4 I will explain it to you and give you the necessary apparatus."[6]

Rose Paget was happy to accept J. J.'s offer. Their meetings started out as scientific discussions. They began getting together more and more often. Soon the student and the professor had to admit that they weren't really spending all their time on science. They were in love. On January 2, 1890, J. J. and Rose were wed. It was the beginning of what would become a long and happy marriage.

That same year, J. J. started a friendly meeting group for fellow scientists and students called the Cavendish Physical Society. It had no rules and no requirements for membership. It normally met once every two weeks. Sometimes one or two items of different members' research were discussed, and sometimes there'd just be a general chat about physics. Mrs. Thomson would usually serve tea at these gatherings, making the gatherings seem even friendlier.

Meanwhile, even though he was truly in love with his new wife, J. J. had to concentrate on his work. When he was working on his own research, he liked to work at home in his own office, sitting in a chair that had once belonged to James Clerk Maxwell. Seated at his desk, J. J. would scribble away on pieces of scrap paper, making note after note until he knew what he wanted to put down in final form. He wasn't a neat person when it came to his papers. That often meant a good deal of frantic searching through all the scraps of paper to find the ones that he wanted. But once J. J. was ready for the final version of a paper or a book, he put his thoughts down on paper in a nice, clear handwriting.

He kept publishing, turning out book after book on science. None of them were for everyday readers, and their titles certainly weren't catchy. But they reached the scientists and students who wanted and needed them. In 1892 his *Notes on Recent Researches in Electricity and Magnetism* was published. Between 1893 and 1894, J. J. co-authored a four-volume textbook of physics called *Properties of Matter* with another professor, J. H. Poynting. In 1895, *Elements of the Mathematical Theory of Electricity* was published. His next book—based on a series of lectures he gave during a visit to the United States in 1896—was *Discharge of Electricity through Gases*, and it appeared in 1897.

That same year he announced a discovery that would eventually shake the scientific community to its roots.

Princeton University

When J. J. wasn't doing research or teaching, he liked to relax and have fun. He had a good sense of humor and loved to tell jokes and laugh at other people's jokes, and even liked to make up funny rhymes for his students.

A major part of his life was his family: his wife and his two children, George and Joan. J. J. spent as much time with them as possible, playing with the children and encouraging them to enjoy learning.

Sometimes J. J. would go on long walks in the country, either alone or with his friends or family. The area around Cambridge is a nice place for hikes. It is hilly, with farmland and some forests. He enjoyed the scenery even in winter. J. J. saw beauty in the bare branches of the trees in his winter walks.

Like many English people, J. J. enjoyed gardening. Although he admitted he wasn't very good at growing plants, he did manage to maintain a lovely garden. He would schedule visits to admire other people's beautiful gardens every year. He enjoyed any chance to see rare plants. J. J. even said that if he had a second life, he'd be a botanist—someone who studies plants.

As an important scientist, J. J. was frequently invited to meetings and conferences. He would take his wife and children with him, and make vacations out of the trips. The Thomson family went to America and Canada on these visits that were part business, part pleasure. In 1896, for instance, J. J. came to America to give four lectures at Princeton University in New Jersey. This gave him a chance to give his family a little vacation. J. J. liked the Americans, enjoying their freedom and (to someone from England) easy-going ways.

J. J. was also a sports fan. He enjoyed watching the Cambridge University teams compete against other universities in the English sports of rugby and cricket.

27

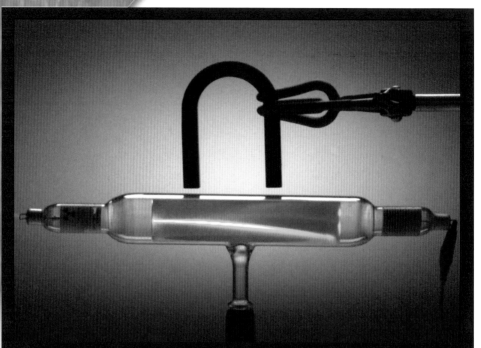

The photograph shows a cathode ray tube with a magnet bending the light path. J. J. used cathode ray tubes similar to the one above to aid in his discovery of the electron.

4

Breaking the Atom

For many centuries, scientists believed that everything in the world was made up of combinations of four basic elements: earth, air, fire and water. This belief was formulated around 350 B.C. by Aristotle, a Greek philosopher. In the latter part of the 18th century, a French scientist named Antoine Lavoisier replaced Aristotle's system with a different definition of elements. He identified more than 20, such as iron, oxygen, gold and sulfur. In 1803, an English chemist named John Dalton proposed a radical theory. He said that elements were made up of tiny atoms, a word that came from a Greek root which means "that which cannot be broken down any further." Every atom of a particular element was identical to other atoms in that element. They were different from atoms of other elements. The thing that distinguished them was what Dalton called their "atomic weight." An atom of gold, for example, weighed more than an atom of sulfur.

As often happens when someone proposes a new way of looking at things, many scientists disagreed with him. But eventually his theory became accepted.

Another thing that was accepted was that atoms really were indivisible. Even though they were far too small to be seen, even

William Crookes was an English physicist. Like J. J., he was curious about the nature of cathode rays. His invention is called the "Crookes Tubes."

with the highest powered microscopes that existed during the era, scientists felt confident that they were solid spheres.

Studying atoms became one of the main activities of scientists in the nineteenth century. It had quickly become apparent that atoms had electrical charges. Many scientists turned their attention to the study of the relationship between atoms and electricity.

In 1855, a German glassblower, Heinrich Geissler, invented a small glass tube from which air could be pumped to create a vacuum. Four years later, Geissler's friend Julius Plücker used those tubes to study electric currents. He sealed two terminals inside the tube. One terminal was called a cathode and had a negative electrical charge. The other was called an anode. It had a positive charge. When he sent a current of electricity between the two terminals, it created a glowing stream of rays of light. Eventually scientists gave the name of cathode rays to this glowing stream.

About 1875, an English physicist named William Crookes improved on Geissler's design. The "Crookes Tubes," as they were called, made it much easier to study cathode rays. But no one was sure what cathode rays were. Most German physicists claimed that cathode rays were caused by vibrations of the ether, a weightless substance that in the nineteenth century was thought to fill all space. Cathode rays weren't ordinary light but some strange kind of waves. British and French physicists disagreed. They claimed that cathode rays consisted of tiny electrified particles. These particles would have to be very tiny, since no one could actually see them.

J. J. studied the mystery of the cathode rays for years. At first he worked alone. Starting in 1895, he had an assistant, fellow physicist Ernest Rutherford. He realized that the first step in solving the mystery was a better cathode tube. The existing ones didn't create a true vacuum. Without a true vacuum, the air left in the tube could affect the experiment.

After trial and error, J. J. designed and built a better cathode tube. Now he could create a true vacuum. This enabled him to get accurate results with his experiments. Soon he noticed that the cathode rays could be moved by electric fields. Now he knew he was onto something really interesting. What was going on? J. J. wanted to see if, by bending the rays with a magnet, he could separate the electric charge from the rays.

Sure enough, he found that the cathode rays bent in an electric field. That meant that they were particles rather than waves. Because they were particles, they had mass, or weight. Their mass was quite small, but it could be measured. In the early months of 1897, J. J. realized that there was something truly amazing about the particles he was measuring. They had less mass, or weight, than the atoms they were a part of.

How could these mysterious particles be lighter than their atoms? There was only one possible conclusion: There really was something smaller than the atom. The atom wasn't solid after all. J. J. had just found one of the pieces that make up an atom.

J. J. realized that his first finding might have been an accident. A scientific experiment must be able to be repeated and give the same results if it is accurate. J. J. tried the experiment again, and he had the same results. He tried different types of gas in the tube instead of a vacuum, and got the same results. He tried other types

Ernest Rutherford was one of J. J.'s students and assistants. He became a famous scientist in his own right. Rutherford discovered the correct shape of the atom.

of metals in the design of the cathode tube, and still got the same results.

There wasn't any mistake. Now he could safely state that all atoms were made up of smaller pieces.

J. J. published his findings in a paper he called simply "Cathode Rays." He read the paper before the Royal Institution of Great Britain, one of the country's most important science organizations, on April 30, 1897. He explained that the intense electrical field in his cathode tube resulted in the subdividing of atoms into tiny particles, which he called corpuscles. The motion of these corpuscles was what made up the current of electricity. He claimed that this subdividing of atoms was true of all kinds of elements.

Other scientists weren't so sure about the accuracy of his claims. The whole thing seemed too strange to them. They insisted that everyone knew the atom couldn't be divided!

J. J. later wrote, "At first there were very few who believed in the existence of these bodies smaller than atoms. I was even told...by a distinguished physicist...that he thought I had been 'pulling their legs.'"[1]

J. J. knew that he hadn't been mistaken. And he certainly hadn't been trying to pull a practical joke on the other scientists. He kept on performing his experiments and reporting on them. By 1899, other scientists had successfully tried the experiments themselves. They had to admit that he was right. The atom wasn't solid. It really was made up of smaller pieces.

If an atom wasn't solid, the next mystery was what did it look like. J. J. himself wasn't sure, so he continued his research into the twentieth century. On March 10, 1904, he delivered a paper, "On the Structure of the Atom," to the Royal Institution. In the paper, he discussed what the atom might actually be like. He said, "We suppose that the atom consists of a number of corpuscles moving about in a sphere of uniform positive electrification: the problems we have to solve are (1) what would be the structure of such an atom, i.e. how would the corpuscles arrange themselves in the sphere; and (2) what properties would this structure confer upon the atom."[2] Since this is a somewhat technical explanation, J. J. thought of a way to make it clearer. He said that the inside of an atom was similar to plum pudding with raisins. The raisins were the corpuscles. Their negative charge was balanced by the positive charge of the pudding. This image led to a joke asking what J. J. Thomson's favorite food was. The right answer, of course, was plum pudding.

Two years later, J. J. was awarded the Nobel Prize in physics for his findings. He gave a summary of his work in his acceptance speech, still referring to the particles he had discovered as corpuscles. By then, he was almost alone in continuing to use this terminology. In 1891, an Irish scientist named George Johnstone Storey had used the term "electron" to refer to the fundamental unit of electricity. When J. J.'s fellow scientists decided his theory was correct, they transferred Storey's term and used it to describe the tiny particles J. J. had discovered. J. J. waited until 1913 to adopt it.

By then, his former student Ernest Rutherford had put forth a different model of the atom. It wasn't plum pudding. Rutherford demonstrated that an atom looks something like a tiny solar system with a central sun and planets. It has a small nucleus, a round core, in the center. Electrons orbit around the nucleus.

Though Rutherford had proved that J. J. was wrong about the structure of the atom, his model depended on J. J.'s groundbreaking research. This research also led to the many exciting developments in the new field of nuclear physics in the twentieth century.

J. J. himself had no idea that his discovery would ever be of any importance to anyone other than scientists. His favorite toast was said to be, "To the electron-may it never be of any use to anybody."[3] With his well-known sense of humor, J. J. may not have intended for people to take his toast seriously. So many elements of modern life are totally dependent on electricity, which consists of electrons in motion. His discovery has proved to be of use to people everywhere.

Electrons and More

Electron comes from the Greek word elektron, which means amber. Amber is fossilized resin, the sap of pine trees and other evergreen plants. The Greeks knew that when amber was rubbed with a dry cloth, it would create what we now call static electricity. It could then draw lightweight objects such as pieces of cloth towards it.

At the end of the sixteenth century, an English doctor named William Gilbert studied magnetism and the natural attraction of amber. He called this attraction electricity after the Greek word for amber.

William Gilbert

After J. J. Thomson's discoveries, scientists knew that subatomic particles like the electron existed. When Ernest Rutherford discovered the existence of the nucleus, he called the subatomic particles that were located there protons. They were much larger than electrons. It soon became evident that there had to be something else in the nucleus. In 1932, English physicist James Chadwick—a student of Rutherford's—identified that something else. It was the neutron, a particle about the same size as a proton but without an electric charge.

The division of the atom doesn't stop there. By the end of the twentieth century, scientists learned that protons and neutrons are made up of even smaller particles. They found a name for these truly tiny particles: quark. The term comes from Finnegan's Wake, an odd book by author James Joyce: "Three quarks for Muster Mark!/Sure he hasn't got much of a bark/And sure any he has it's all beside the mark."[4] Actually, Joyce didn't make up the word. Quark is an old English word meaning to caw. Whatever its original meaning, quark now refers to subatomic particles. There are six kinds of quarks: up, down, top, bottom, strange, and charm. Those names don't mean anything. Scientists just picked words at random so they'd have something to call them. They call the particle that glues quarks together by another funny name: it's a gluon (pronounced GLUE-on).

Is there anything smaller than the quark? No one knows—not yet, at any rate.

35

In addition to the Nobel Prize, J. J. received many awards from scientific organizations. He was also the recipient of various honorary doctorate degrees from universities around the world.

5

Afterwards

The Nobel Prize wasn't the only sign of respect for J. J.'s work. During the early years of the twentieth century, J. J. received more and more honors for his work. In 1902, he received the Royal and Hughes Medals from England and the Hodgkins Medal from the United States. He was knighted by King Edward VII in 1908, becoming Sir Joseph John Thomson.

He continued to share his knowledge with his fellow scientists. In 1907, he published two more books, *The Structure of Light and The Corpuscular Theory of Matter.* In 1913, J. J. published still another book, *Rays of Positive Electricity.* It all seemed a perfect way for a scientist to live: a happy family, a good workplace, and plenty of good conversation with other scientists.

Then in 1914, the world changed forever. World War I began. This terrible war has been given several other names, including the Great War and the War to End All Wars. (Unfortunately, it wasn't the last war, and it didn't end all wars.) It was called a World War because so many countries fought in it. England was one of those countries, fighting against Germany, which had already declared war on France and invaded Belgium. (The United States eventually joined England and France in the fight against Germany, but not until 1917.)

J. J. served as a scientific advisor to the English government during the war. He also served as a member of the Board of Invention and Research, which was created by the English government in 1915 to let scientists help the English war effort. J. J. stayed on as the Cavendish Laboratory Professor despite the war. The war caused major changes in the lives of the Cavendish Laboratory scientists. Those who stayed at the laboratory were forced by the British government to give up all research except for research that could be used in the war. The laboratory also housed British soldiers.

J. J. never lost his sense of humor during those difficult times. He wrote about the strange and maybe even crazy people who had contacted him with their weird ideas on how to end the war. J. J. had to deal with a man who claimed to have built a perpetual motion machine. This was a device that—at least in theory—would run forever, without needing any fuel. He also heard from a woman "who was much upset by a bad smell and thinks it might be bottled up and used" as a war weapon.

In spite of the distractions and turmoil caused by the war, the scientific community in England tried to carry on life as normal. One result was that J. J. was elected President of the prestigious Royal Society in 1915.

The war ended in 1918 with the defeat of Germany. Life in the Cavendish Laboratory returned to normal. Its scientists were free to begin research on other subjects than war. In the same year, J. J. was chosen to be Master—or head—of Trinity College. In 1919, finally overwhelmed with too many responsibilities, he resigned as Cavendish Laboratory Professor.

In 1923, J. J. published another book, *The Electron in Chemistry*. By the 1930s, J. J. was given more awards, as well as a whole list of honorary doctorate degrees from universities around the world. No longer young, he decided the time had come to publish his autobiography. Entitled *Recollections and Reflections*, it was published in 1936. J. J. also had the thrill of seeing his son George win the Nobel Prize for physics the following year.

J. J. continued to be Master of Trinity College, running things with his usual skill and good humor, but time was running out for him. He died on August 30, 1940, at the age of 83. His ashes were buried in Westminster Abbey, not far from the grave of another great scientist, Sir Isaac Newton.

In addition to J. J.'s contributions to science, he started a highly successful program of experimental

Bill Gates is the founder of Microsoft. He is also a fan of the sciences. He named one of the main roads in the Microsoft complex after J. J.

physics during his time as Cavendish Laboratory Professor. Many important experiments took place and the graduates included no fewer than seven winners of the Nobel Prize and twenty-seven fellows, or honored members, of the Royal Society.

People haven't forgotten J. J. Thomson. Bill Gates, chairman of the giant software manufacturer Microsoft, is well aware of J. J.'s scientific achievements. When he was building the Microsoft complex of buildings in Cambridge, Gates named one of the roads the J. J. Thomson Avenue. The University of Essex in England honored J. J. by establishing the J. J. Thomson Premium, a yearly science award for research scientists. There is also a Thomson Medal, named in his honor, awarded once every three years to scientists by the International Mass Spectrometry Society.

Like Father, Like Son

George Thomson

George Thomson seems to have inherited both his father's intelligence and his fascination with science. Like his father, he attended Trinity College, where he studied mathematics and physics. His dad (J. J.) was his professor for a year.

When England entered World War I in 1914, George became an army officer and served in France. English military officials soon realized who he was. They sent him back to England to work on the new science of military aviation, designing war planes. Actually, all kinds of aviation were still new. The first flight, by the Wright Brothers in Kitty Hawk, North Carolina, had only been in 1903. England was one of the first countries to use airplanes in war.

After the war, George lectured at Cambridge, and continued his research in physics. In 1924 he married Kathleen Buchanan. They had a family of four children, two boys and two girls. Soon after his marriage, George became Professor of Natural Philosophy at the University of Aberdeen in Scotland, where physics was still called "natural philosophy." He taught there for eight years.

At Aberdeen, George carried out experiments on electrons, proving that they could travel like waves even though they were particles. In 1937, he was rewarded for his work with the Nobel Prize. J. J. was still alive then, and was very proud of his son. Like his father, George was also made a knight.

In 1939, George became interested in the developing science of nuclear physics, and worked with American scientists on the development of the atomic bomb. After the war, he became more interested in the peaceful uses of nuclear power.

In addition to writing J. J. Thomson and the Cavendish Laboratory in His Day, a book about his father, George wrote scientific books and articles. He also wrote two books for non-scientists: The Atom and the Foreseeable Future and The Inspiration of Science.

He died in 1975.

Chronology

1856   Born on December 18

1871   Enters Owens College

1876   Enters Trinity College, Cambridge University

1877   Publishes first scientific paper on mathematics

1880   Graduates from Trinity College

1882   Wins the Adams Prize for his paper, "A Treatise on the Motion of Vortex Rings"

1884   Becomes Cavendish Professor and head of the Cavendish Laboratory at Cambridge University

1886   Publishes his first book, *Application of Dynamics to Physics and Chemistry*

1890   Marries Rose Paget

1892   Publishes *Notes on Recent Researches in Electricity and Magnetism*

1896   Travels to the United States to give a series of lectures at Princeton University

1897   Discovers the electron, which he calls a "corpuscle"

1906   Wins the Nobel Prize in Physics

1908   Is knighted by King Edward VII

1918   Named Master of Trinity College

1919   Resigns as Cavendish Professor

1937   J. J.'s son, Sir George Thomson, wins the Nobel Prize

1940   Dies on August 30

Timeline in History

ca. 600 B.C.	Greek philosopher Thales of Miletus studies magnetism and the static electric aspects of amber; the Greek word for amber, elektron, is the source of the modern words electron" and electricity.
ca. 500 B.C.	Greek philosopher Pythagoras discovers that science problems can be worked out by mathematics.
ca. 460 B.C.	Greek scholar and politician Empedocles describes a form of the law of conservation of energy and writes about the four basic elements of nature.
300 B.C.	Greek mathematician Euclid sets up perhaps the first school of mathematics, in Alexandria, Egypt.
ca. 1260	English friar Roger Bacon studies magnetism, and may have devised a true compass.
1600	English scholar William Gilbert publishes *De Magnete*, about magnetism and electricity, and coins the word *electricitas*, or electricity.
1704	English scientist Sir Isaac Newton publishes his book *Opticks*, which puts forward the particle theory of light.
1744	Russian scientist Mikhail Vasilievich Lomonosov gives the first description of heat as a form of motion.
1752	Benjamin Franklin proves that lightning is electricity.
1800	Italian scientist Alessandro Volta produces the first electrical battery
1819	Danish scientist Hans Christian Oersted proves that electricity generates a magnetic field, linking the two forces.
1821	English scientist Michael Faraday proves that magnetism also exerts a force over electricity, and that electrical energy can be used for moving machinery.
1827	France scientist Andre Marie Ampere publishes the mathematical formula regarding electrodynamics, which becomes known as Ampere's Law.
1832	French inventor Hippolyte Pixii invents the first practical electric generator.

42

Timeline in History (Cont'd)

1845	English scientist James Joule formulates Joule's Law, which describes the way that an electric current produces heat.
1859	German scientist Julius Plücker discovers cathode rays.
1873	Scottish scientist James Clerk Maxwell publishes his *Treatise on Electricity and Magnetism*, in which he proves the theory of electromagnetism.
1900	German physicist Max Planck develops a formula linking the energy of radiation to its frequency.
1911	British scientist Ernest Rutherford develops a model of an atom with a central nucleus surrounded by electrons.
1913	Danish physicist Niels Bohr develops the first model of an atom with quantum energy.
1927	English physicist Charles Thomson Wilson is awarded the Nobel Prize in physics for inventing the Wilson cloud chamber, an instrument for tracking atomic particles.
1932	German physicist Werner Heisenberg receives the Nobel Prize in physics for his work on quantum mechanics, the theoretical working of the universe on the subatomic level.
1935	British physicist James Chadwick receives the Nobel Prize in physics for his discovery of the neutron.
1953	James Watson from America and Francis Crick of England develop the double helix model of DNA.
1963	Physicist Maria Goeppert-Meyer becomes the first American woman to receive the Nobel Prize for physics for her studies of atomic nuclei.
1969	The scanning electron microscope is developed, allowing three-dimensional pictures of cells to be produced.
1982	Swiss physicist Heinrich Rohrer and German physicist Gerd Binnig invent the scanning tunneling microscope which can provide images of individual atoms.
2004	The Nobel Prize in Physics is awarded to scientists David J. Gross, H. David Politzer, and Frank Wilczek for their work on quarks.
2005	The United Nations declares this the World Year of Physics.

Chapter Notes

Chapter 1   The Professor Who Liked Questions

1. Although the story has been fictionalized a little, it is a true one. J. J. described the incident in a letter he wrote soon afterward. We don't know the boy's name, but J. J. did, indeed, sit with him and answer all his questions.

Chapter 2   The Bookseller's Son

1. J. J. Thomson, *Recollections and Reflections*, (London: Bell, 1936.)

2. Ibid.

Chapter 3   Professor Thomson

1. "J. J. Thomson," Cambridge University Department of Physics, http://www.phy.cam.ac.uk/cavendish/history/electron/description.php

2. R. J. Strutt, *The Life of Sir J. J. Thomson, O.M.* (Cambridge, England: Cambridge University Press, 1942).

3. J. J. Thomson, *Recollections and Reflections* (London: Bell, 1936).

4. From "A Look Inside the Atom," http://www.aip.org/history/electron/jjhome.htm

5. J. J. 's parody is considered to be in the public domain; that is, a song that is free to be sung by anyone. His parody, and many others by scientists having fun, can be found at http://www.mnsta.org/links/songs.htm

6. George Paget Thomson, *J. J. Thomson and the Cavendish Laboratory in His Day* (New York: Doubleday & Company, 1965).

Chapter 4   Breaking the Atom

1. J. J. Thomson, *Recollections and Reflections* (London: Bell, 1936).

2. J. J. Thomson, "On the Structure of the Atom," *Philosophical Magazine*, March, 1904.

3. The Discovery of the Electron, http://www.pbs.org/transistor/science/events/electron.html

4. James Joyce, *Finnegan's Wake* (New York: Penguin Books, 1976).

Chapter 5   Afterward

1. E.A. Davis and I.J. Falconer, *J. J. Thomson and the Discovery of the Electron* (London, Taylor & Francis, 1997).

44

Glossary

amber — (AM-burr)—fossilized resin.

atom — (A-tum)—the smallest particle of an element that keeps the properties of that element.

cathode tube — (KA-thode TOOB)—a glass tube from which air is removed to create a vacuum and through which a beam of electrons is passed.

corpuscle — (KOHR-puh-sull)—a tiny particle; J. J. Thomson's name for the electron.

electrodynamism — (ee-leck-troe-DYE-nam-izm)—the interaction among electricity, magnetism and machinery.

electromagnetism — (ee-leck-troe-MAG-nuh-tizm)—a magnetic force produced by an electrical current.

electron — (ee-LECK-trahn)—a negatively charged particle that circles an atom's nucleus.

energy — (EH-nur-jee)—the capacity to do work or produce heat.

kinetic energy — (kuh-NEH-tick EH-nur-jee)—the energy of motion.

Nobel Prize — (no-BELL PRIZE)—A major international prize awarded every year for achievements in chemistry, economics, literature, peace, physics, and physiology and medicine.

nucleus — (NEW-klee-us)—the central, positively charged core of the atom.

potential energy — (poe-TEN-shul EH-nur-jee)—stored energy.

subatomic particles — (sub-uh-TAW-mic PAR-tih-culs)—bits of matter or energy that are smaller than an atom.

vacuum — (VA-kyum)—a completely empty space.

45

For Further Reading

For Young Adults

Goldstein, Natalie. *The Nature of the Atom: Great Scientific Questions and the Scientists Who Answered Them*. New York: Rosen Publishing, 2001.

Snedden, Robert. *Energy*. Chicago: Heinemann Library, 1999.

Stwertka, Albert. *World of Atoms & Quarks*. New York: 21st Century Books, 1997.

Works Consulted

Abbott, David, ed. *The Biographical Dictionary of Scientists: Physicists*. New York: Peter Bedrick Books, 1984.

Buchwald, Jed Z. and Andrew Warwick, eds. *Histories of the Electron*. Cambridge, Massachusetts: MIT Press, 2001.

Dahl, Per F. *Flash of the Cathode Rays: A History of J. J. Thomson's Electrons*. Bristol and Philadelphia: Institute of Physics Publishing, 1997.

Davis, E. A. and I. J. Falconer. *J. J. Thomson and the Discovery of the Electron*. London: Taylor & Francis, 1997.

Gundersen, P. Erik. *The Handy Physics Answer Book*. Detroit and London: Visible Ink Press, 1999.

Harman, Peter and Simon Mitton. *Cambridge Scientific Minds*. Cambridge: Cambridge University Press, 2002.

Joyce, James. *Finnegan's Wake*. New York: Penguin Books, 1976.

Kim, Dong-Won. *Leadership and Creativity: A History of the Cavendish Laboratory, 1871-1919*. Dodrecht, New York and London: Kluwer Academic Publishers, 2002.

Leiter, Darryl J. *A to Z of Physicists*. New York: Facts on File, 2003.

McGrath, Kimberly. *World of Physics, 2 volumes*. Detroit: The Gale Group, 2001.

Magill, Frank N. *The Nobel Prize Winners: Physics, Volume 1, 1901-1937*. Pasadena, CA and Englewood Cliffs, NJ: Salem Press, 1989.

Morgan, Bryan. *Men and Discoveries in Electricity*. London: John Murray, 1952.

For Further Reading (Cont'd)

Strutt, R. J. *The Life of Sir J. J. Thomson, O. M.* Cambridge: Cambridge University Press, 1942.

Thomson, George Paget. *J. J. Thomson and the Cavendish Laboratory in His Day*. New York: Doubleday & Company, 1965.

Thomson, J. J. *Notes on Recent Researches in Electricity and Magnetism*. Oxford: The Clarendon Press, 1893.

Thomson, J. J. "On the Structure of the Atom," *Philosophical Magazine*, March 1904, p. 237-265.

Thomson, J. J. *Recollections and Reflections*. London: Bell, 1936.

On the Internet

The Americam Institute of Physics: *A Look inside the Atom*.
   http://www.aip.org/history/electron/jjhome.htm

Cambridge University Department of Physics: *J. J. Thomson*.
   http://www.phy.cam.ac.uk/cavendish/history/electron/description.php

The Nobel Prize: *J. J. Thomson*.
   http://www.nobel.se/physics/laureates/1906/thomson-bio.html

PBS: *Discovery of the Electron*.
   http://www.pbs.org/transistor/science/events/electron.html

The Third Millenium Online: *Discovery of the Electron*, "Cathode Rays."
   http://www.3rd1000.com/history/electrons.htm

Vocal Source

Science Museum: *Archive Recordings of J. J. Thomson*
   http://www.sciencemuseum.org.uk/on-line/electron/section2/recording.asp

Index